A BOOT UP

THE HAMPSHIRE HANGERS

Mike Cope

First published in Great Britain in 2010

The author would like to thank the Edward Thomas Estate
for permission to quote from his poetry and *Country Walking*
magazine for permission to use extracts from previously published routes.

British Library Cataloguing-in-Publication Data
A CIP record for this title is available from the British Library

ISBN 978 0 85710 018 4

PiXZ Books
Halsgrove House, Ryelands Industrial Estate,
Bagley Road, Wellington, Somerset TA21 9PZ
Tel: 01823 653777
Fax: 01823 216796
email: sales@halsgrove.com

An imprint of Halstar Ltd, part of the Halsgrove group of companies
Information on all Halsgrove titles is available at: www.halsgrove.com

Printed and bound in China by Toppan Leefung Printing Ltd

Contents

How to use this book

The Area

The East Hampshire Hangers are remnants of ancient woodland that cling to the steep slopes of the Chalk and Upper Greensand scarps between Langrish and Binsted. The term 'hanger' is derived from an old English word 'hangra', meaning a wooded slope. These hangers have survived because the land has always been too steep to cultivate, and not easily accessible to livestock.

Between Langrish and Steep, the Chalk and Upper Greensand scarps effectively merge, with the Greensand creating the lower and gentler part of the slope. But further north, as the two escarpments diverge, a 'plateau' or 'terrace' of Upper Greensand is formed, which outcrops at the foot of the steep chalk scarp. Between Steep and Selborne, this terrace is scalloped with streams and rivers cutting through the Upper Greensand in relatively deep valleys.

The Chalk Hangers are steep, wooded slopes, more clearly defined to the south of Selborne, and form the dramatic western edge of the Upper Greensand terrace. The scarp twists and writhes around Steep, where the hanging woods plunge into a deep, mysterious combe. Prominent chalk escarpments and hangers are to be found around Oakshott, Hawkley, Noar Hill and Selborne - where the terrace is about one mile across.

The Upper Greensand Hangers are more dominant in the landscape to the north of Selborne — particularly from Wick Hill to East Worldham — and form the less-imposing eastern edge of the terrace. In general, the views from the Upper Greensand Hangers are more local and intimate, but where landslips have occurred, the scarp slopes can be almost vertical. The Chalk and Upper Greensand Hangers effectively form two steps down from the high chalk plateau onto the floor of the Weald.

The Hampshire Hangers landscape has inspired many writers and artists. Selborne is associated with the 18th century curate Gilbert White, author of *The Natural History of Selborne*, and the founding father of natural history recording. Steep was where Edward Thomas found the inspiration and material for the majority of his poetry. Jane Austen spent the last eight years of her life at Chawton, writing and revising her great romantic comedies.

A 21 mile long-distance footpath (the Hangers Way), runs through the Hampshire Hangers landscape, from Queen Elizabeth Country Park to Alton.

The Routes

The village of Selborne lies at the heart of the Hampshire Hangers landscape. Six of the routes are along the Chalk Hangers to the south of the village and the remaining four are along the Upper Greensand Hangers to the north and southeast.

All routes are either circular, or a figure of eight design. They range from 4½ - 9½ miles and are graded from one to three boots — from easy to the more challenging.

Standard grid references are given for accurate location of starting points using an OS map (or mapping websites, such as www.multimap.com). A postcode or 'nearest postcode' is also given to locate the starting point with the aid of an in-car Sat Nav system. If the starting point is not near a postal address, then the 'nearest postcode' may be some distance away from the actual starting point.

The Maps

Although a thorough description of each walk is given and a sketch map provided, it is advisable to take with you a compass (or Sat Nav) and a detailed OS map of the area, should you stray from the route or are forced to cut it short. Conveniently, the whole area is covered by the 133 and 144 OS Explorer maps.

Key to Symbols Used

Level of difficulty:

Easy 🐾

Fair 🐾🐾

More challenging 🐾🐾🐾

Map symbols:

🚗	Park & start
	Tarred Road
- - - - -	Footpath
■	Building / Town
🍺	Pub
▲	Landmark
+	Church
▦	Railway Line
	River or stream
	Hanger

Walk Locations

10 Binsted

East Worldham

8 Chawton

9

Oakhanger

Selborne **7**

6

4

Greatham

5

2

3 Hawkley

1 Steep

☐ Chalk
☐ Upper Greensand (Malmstone)
■ Gault Clay
☐ Lower Greensand

1 Steep and Ashford Hanger

A 5½ mile circuit, in the heart of Edward Thomas country, with steep ascents and breath-taking views

Level: 🥾 🥾
Length: 5½ miles (9km)
Terrain: Some fairly arduous climbs up Chalk and Upper Greensand Hangers
Park and start: Steep church
Start ref: SU 746253
Postcode (nearest): GU32 2DD
Public transport: Countryliner bus (route 95) from Petersfield station to Steep (Bedales school)
Refreshments and facilities: The Cricketers, Steep

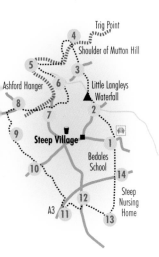

On a hillside north of Steep, lies a sarcen stone, set up as a memorial to the poet Edward Thomas. This area, north of Petersfield, is where Edward Thomas found the inspiration and material for the majority of his poetry. The Shoulder of Mutton Hill is one of the steepest climbs in the whole range of hangers, and is recognized from a great distance by its grassy clearing, framed by a dark mass of ancient yews. Further west, the beech and yew hanging woods, plunge into a dark, mysterious combe, where mists sometimes spiral, as from a cauldron.

THIS HILLSIDE
IS DEDICATED TO THE MEMORY OF
EDWARD THOMAS

Octagonal plaque on Poet's Stone

Steep and Ashford Hanger

The Shoulder of Mutton Hill

1 Follow the Hangers Way fingerpost through the recreational area opposite **Steep church** and into woodland. Proceed along the slowly descending path, until it emerges from woodland, with a field on the right hand side. The wooded slopes of **Ashford Hanger** and the **Shoulder of Mutton Hill**, with its sweep of chalk grassland, now rise beckoningly above you. Keep following the path until you reach a rusty metal kissing gate.

2 Turn right along road and at the first right hand bend, keep ahead over a footbridge by a waterfall. Go left at the T-junction, along a newly cut path, through **Little Langleys** conservation area. Pass another scenic pool, as the path performs a zig zag and then merges with an untarred lane.

Climbing the Shoulder of Mutton Hill

Admiring the view from the Shoulder of Mutton Hill

3 Turn right at the road, and then left, 50 metres later, along a field edge. Cross a stile into **Ashford Hangers**, and at the junction, take the rising path. As you ascend the steep flight of steps cut

Just thirty months before his untimely death on the Western Front, Edward Thomas started writing poetry. What he left behind was a canon of some 140 poems, composed in a burst of creativity, including 'Adlestrop' and 'Old Man'– two of his best-known verses.

into the hillside, you may recall the Edward Thomas line: 'fast beat my heart at sight of the tall slope'. Half way up, there is a bench and large memorial stone, and from here you can savour 'sixty miles of South Downs at one glance'. Continue up the scarp slope past sombre yews, towering beeches and the occasional juniper bush.

4 Go through a wooden barrier and then turn immediately left down a well-trodden path. Exposed tree roots cling precariously to the chalk hanger, as the path descends gradually. Maintain direction at the fork on a downhill path.

The Edward Thomas memorial stone

Hangers Way signpost

5 At the next junction, turn obliquely left along the **Hangers Way**. Keep ahead on the main track, ignoring all turnoffs. When a wooden handrail appears, the track may start to get muddier — so take care. Pass a babbling brook (**Ashford stream**) and then a pond on the left.

> *Each year, the Edward Thomas Fellowship stages a commemorative Birthday Walk around Steep, on the anniversary of the poet's birth.*

6 Turn right at the road, and follow it as it winds uphill. Go right at the T-junction, near **Island Farm**, and keep going until you reach the main road.

7 Go right at the main road and then left, 50 metres later, up an off-road cycle trail. This second ascent of **Ashford Hanger** is longer and more drawn out than the first — and there's no poetry to console you either!

8 At the crest of the hill, bear left along the road, past **Stoner Hill Farm**. Before a triangular junction, go left over a stile and along the left hand edge of a field. Climb a rickety stile into woodland, and then fork immediately right down a narrow, ill-trodden path through the hanger. At the bottom, another track merges from the left. After 30 metres, go left down a man-made staircase, and cross a stile to emerge from woodland.

(9) Here you encounter a fabulous panorama: the whale-back humps of the South Downs appear on the right, then stretch ahead into the distance; and the hanger behind you continues south-westerly towards Langrish and East Meon. Continue across the field towards the double telegraph pole. Bear left at the next fingerpost and then keep to the right hand edge of the field. Cross a stile and follow path diagonally across a field.

View of South Downs from Ashford Hanger

Hanger stretching towards Langrish

(10) At the road, go left and then bear right after 30 metres, over a stile. Cross another stile and proceed along enclosed path. Go over tarmac drive and maintain direction along right hand edge of field. Cross a sunken lane, climb a stile and keep to left hand edge of field. Climb another stile near a mobile phone mast and follow winding path to footbridge over the A3.

11 Go left along enclosed path, cross a stile and then bear right along tarred lane near horse paddocks. Cross another stile and when you reach a main road, turn left.

12 Take the first right along **Bell Hill Ridge road**. When the tarmac runs out, keep ahead along enclosed path.

The grounds of Bedales School

13 At the next junction, bear left along the Hangers Way. When you reach a road, turn left along it, and keep ahead at the next right hand bend, near **Steep House Nursing Home**.

14 Re-cross the A3 at the footbridge, then go immediately right. Keep ahead along an enclosed path, past the playing fields of **Bedales School**, until you reach **Steep church**.

Steep church

In the church of All Saints, Steep there are two memorial windows, designed and engraved by Laurence Whistler, to commemorate the centenary of Edward Thomas's birth. The windows were dedicated in 1978 by the poet R.S.Thomas.

2 **The Warren and Happersnapper Hanger**

Explore hanging woods that tumble down the slopes of a deep chalk combe on this 5¼ mile circuit

The White Horse Inn - at 235 metres above sea level - is Hampshire's highest pub. In 1914, Edward Thomas used it as the setting for one of his finest prose-poems: 'Up in the Wind'. In the latter half of the poem, the 'cockney barmaid' expresses her exasperation for the wind that keeps her awake at night, and her relief when it blows the sign down. The reason for her being there is a chronicle of accidents, personal destinies and demographic shifts. Despite not having a signboard, many manage to find their way to the 'Pub with no name' for the Longest Day Beer Festival, which takes place on the nearest weekend to the Solstice.

Level: 🥾

Length: 5¼ miles (8.5 km)

Terrain: Some slippery descents around The Warren and one arduous ascent up Happersnapper Hanger

Park and start: The White Horse (Pub with no name), Priors Dean

Start ref: SU 714290

Postcode: GU32 1DA

Public transport: None to start, but Countryliner bus (route 95) stops at Warren Corner

Refreshments and facilities: The White Horse (Pub with no name), Priors Dean; the Trooper Inn, Froxfield

Signpost near Hawkley Hanger

Post and empty Frame

12
1
Farm 2
Ragmore Farm
11
Green Lane
The Warren 4
3
10 Trig Point Farm
9
8
5
Farm
6
7

1 With your back to the entrance of the **White Horse pub**, go through a metal gate into field opposite. Turn immediately right and continue through a wooden kissing gate at top of field. Keep to right hand edge of field and negotiate a second kissing gate. Maintain direction across large field and when you reach the boundary of a farm, keep ahead across overgrown area with fence on right.

The White Horse (Pub with no name)

2 Go through a kissing gate and proceed to top right hand corner of cattle field and through another gate. Keep ahead along wide grassy walkway, past work buildings and houses on the right. Eventually there are fields on both sides of the walkway. When you reach a road, go right and then immediately left down Warren Lane.

3 Continue along tree-lined lane past a house (**Foxglen**) on left and then a small parking area on right.

The Warren Nature Reserve

William Cobbett describes his journey to Hawkley, via the Warren, in his book Rural Rides (1830). Before the journey, his friends remonstrated with him about the dangers of breaking his neck down the hanger, which would have been treacherous on horseback.

(4) When you see a semi-circular sign for **The Warren Nature Reserve**, go left into the wood and descend the man-made staircase. At the bottom, go right along path with dark sombre yews on the scarp slope and towering beeches on the left. A shaft of sunlight may occasionally penetrate the sterile ground beneath the yew trees. Eventually you come to another semicircular sign for **The Warren**. Go through a vehicle barrier and then turn left along a sunken lane. When you emerge from the trees, continue along unpaved lane with house (**Doscombe**) on right. The large wood that towers above you is Hawkley Hanger.

Sunken lane down hanger

(5) Turn right at the road and right again at signpost in direction of **Oakshott** and **Wheatham**. Continue past dwellings on left and **Oakshott Farm** on right.

Disused barn near Hawkley Hanger

6 After a few hundred metres, bear right into field, at a wide passing point, with no obvious waymark. Keep to the right hand edge of field past disused farm equipment. Pass dwelling and caravan on left, as track gets progressively steeper. Very soon you will be out of breath, as you negotiate the never-ending ascent through beech woodland.

7 When you see a semi-circular sign for **Happersnapper Hanger**, you can be sure that the worst is over. The track emerges from woodland and passes houses and cattle barns on right. After a few hundred metres you will reach **Honeycritch Cottage**.

Field path near trig point

8 Turn right at fingerpost, opposite cottage, and keep to right hand edge of field. Notice the abundance of flints, which the plough has uncovered, in the soil around you. And if you come in the autumn, look out for the sloes in the hedgerow.

9 Follow the hedge as it turns sharply right and then left and maintain direction past a spinney. Pass a trig point and pause to survey the panorama. Some of the curves of the South Downs should be visible on the distant horizon.

Signpost near Warren Corner

Muddy pools along Green Lane

17

Green Lane is the setting for Edward Thomas's poem 'The Lane'. This heavily-rutted churned-up byway is dead-straight and about a mile long. You can still make out 'the glint of hollies dark in the swollen hedges'.

10 Turn left when you reach a road and at the next T-junction go half right along a by-way, known as **Green Lane** – a heavily-rutted, churned-up track, lined with holly bushes. Stay on it for a mile, and maintain direction when it merges with a metalled lane.

11 Pass **Ragmore Farm** and bear right at the next road junction. Continue to the crossroads, where the cars drive obliviously past the post and empty frame.

12 Keep ahead and then bear right after 250 metres into the driveway of the 'Pub with no name'.

Along Barnet side lane

The empty signboard

3 **Oakshott Hanger and Hawkley**

A 5½ mile figure-of-eight walk through ancient hanger woodland, with panoramic views from Oakshott Hanger

The Hawkley landslip occurred in March 1774, when a considerable proportion of the Upper Greensand Hanger was torn from its place leaving a cliff-like structure resembling the side of a chalk-pit. Gilbert White was ill with a severe cold at the time of the landslip, but relied on reports from his nephew Gibraltar Jack. He wrote in his journal 'About fifty acres of land suffered from this violent convulsion; two houses were entirely destroyed; one end of a new barn was left in ruins; a hanging coppice was changed to a naked rock.' The most likely cause of the subsidence was the weathering of the Malmstone edge, after weeks of snow and torrential rain.

Level: 🌑 🌑
Length: 5½ miles (8.8 km)
Terrain: Steep ascent up Oakshott Hanger; very slippery descent down sunken lane (Down Hanger) – walking boots recommended
Park and start: The Hawkley Inn, Hawkley
Start ref: SU 747291
Postcode: GU33 6NE
Public transport: Bus 252 from Peterfield to Hawkley (very limited service)
Refreshments and facilities: The Hawkley Inn

The Hawkley Inn

HAWKLEY INN
FREE HOUSE

1) From **Hawkley Inn**, go down the lane towards the church and take the first left along **Cheesecombe Farm Lane**.

2) Fork right after a few hundred metres to follow the **Hangers Way**. Continue down enclosed path, past house on left, and follow path as it veers round to right across an open area. Cross (or go round) two stiles with beech woodland on right. Cross double footbridge across Oakshott stream and then another footbridge and stile.

Dilapidated signpost near Hawkley

3 When you reach a road (near **Middle Oakshott Farm**), go right and then immediately left up a wide unmetalled lane. Pass some dwellings, and when the lane runs out, go left over a high stile. Keep to the left hand edge of the field and cross another stile. Steady yourself for a steep, arduous ascent of Oakshott Hanger, which may leave you tired and breathless. At the top, there are spectacular views towards Hawkley church and Noar Hill.

4 Cross two stiles and proceed along the edge of Oakshott Hanger, keeping fence to the right. Cross another stile with towering beeches (and the occasional yew tree) bordering path. Zig zag right and then left, and when you reach the top, climb a high stile to **Old Litten Lane**.

Path along edge of Oakshott Hanger

Panoramic view from Oakshott Hanger

5 Go left along lane (which is usually muddy) and when you reach a cattle shed, fork left along unmetalled lane, with open area on right. The lane starts descending through woodland and after a while, it becomes rutted and very chalky underfoot. Take care through this slippery section. Fields then appear on the right, and the gradient starts to level out. But don't be fooled by this, because very soon, the chalk and clay are back and the lane gets rutted and slippery again.

6 When you reach a road, bear right and then immediately left along an off-road cycle trail. Keep ahead along this tree-lined path and then bear left at the first public foot-path fingerpost.

7 Keep to right hand edge of field and pass some damson bushes. At end of field, go right over a stile along overgrown path. At next junction, go left across field on shoulder of hill and locate concealed stile in top right hand corner. Cross footbridge over stream, pass a small shed, and house on right. Retrace your steps to **Cheesecombe Farm Lane**. When the lane ends, maintain direction across village green to pass the lychgate of **Hawkley church** on the right.

Slippery descent down sunken lane

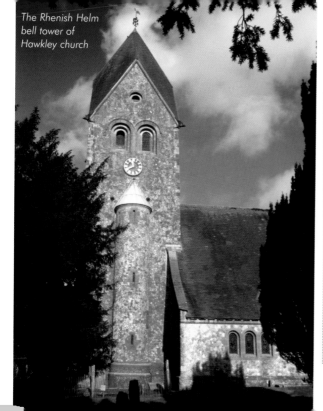

The Rhenish Helm bell tower of Hawkley church

The church of St Peter and St Paul at Hawkley has a distinctive bell tower shaped like a Rhineland helmet. The style of 'Rhenish Helm' was popular in the Rhineland area of Germany in Anglo Saxon times.

8 Maintain direction past **Jolly Robins** on the left. When you reach a crossroads, keep ahead along **Uplands Lane**.

Signpost near Hawkley village

9 Take the first left along a bridleway (near a pond) and keep to right hand edge of field. Lower ground to the right indicates that you are walking along the edge of a hanger. At top right hand corner of field, drop down a small bank to a sunken lane.

10 Turn right and pass farm with a green roof. Fork immediately right, along a descending path. Ignore the next right fork, and keep ahead to kissing gate. Maintain direction across field and enter woodland. Go through kissing gate, and keep following path which bends to the right and passes through a wooded hollow.

Footbridge over Oakshott stream

11 When you see a small information sign, turn sharp right through a kissing gate and across a field. You will soon hear the distant roar of the A3, across fields to the left. Maintain direction along field edge, and go through three gates in quick succession. Enter woodland and continue on rising path through the hanger. Notice the contorted beech trunks on left bank of sunken path. When you reach the top, climb stile

and proceed along left hand edge of field. A landslip occurred here on the Upper Greensand Hanger to the left, in 1774. Go through three metal gates across horse paddocks, and then climb stile to a road.

12 Bear right at the road and take the next left along an enclosed path. When you reach a road, keep ahead towards the Hawkley Inn.

4 Hawkley Hanger and Priors Dean

Mix poetry with English wine on this 4¾ mile walk along Hawkley Hanger

Level: 🥾
Length: 4¾ miles (7.7 km)
Terrain: Undulating, with one moderate descent of Hawkley Hanger; some road walking involved – down quiet lanes
Park and start: Small lay-by opposite Button's Lane (byway)
Start ref: SU 740308
Postcode(nearest): GU34 3SF
Public transport: None to start, but bus 252 (from Petersfield) stops at Hawkley (very limited service)
Refreshments and facilities: The Hawkley Inn, Hawkley

The vineyard at Priors Dean was established in 1988 and the 1.5 acre site is particularly suited to the production of fine white wines. The steep south-facing slope catches the sun, and the surrounding trees give shelter from north and east winds. The Elizabethan manor house at Priors Dean is considerably older, and was the setting for Edward Thomas's 1914 poem 'The Manor Farm'. With its prose rhythms and plain language, it perfectly captures the essence of the English countryside, in this remote corner of East Hampshire.

Map showing the walking route with numbered waypoints. Labels include: Trig Point, Priors Dean Vineyard, Manor Farm, Hawkley Hanger, Hawkley. Waypoints numbered 1–12.

Bent signpost near Button's Lane

25

Looking back along Hawkley Hanger

Priors Dean Vineyard

Priors Dean vineyard is sited on a steep south-facing slope and has a similar chalk soil structure to the Champagne region of France. It is particularly suited to the production of fine white wines, and varieties grown include: Bacchus, Madeleine Angevine, and Seyval Blanc.

① From the layby, take the rising path opposite into woodland. This byway can be rutted and slippery in wet weather, and is flanked by towering beeches with 'graceful pendulous boughs'. As you gain height, there are fabulous views along **Hawkley Hanger**, with Ashford Hanger behind it on the left. Pass **Priors Dean Vineyard**, which is sited on a steep south-facing slope, and particularly suited to the production of fine white wines. In due course, the byway merges with a metalled lane and then bends round to the right.

View of Noar Hill from the top of Button's Lane

② Turn left at the next junction and proceed downhill along a hollow lane. Should you encounter any traffic, there are some passing points to take refuge in. At the bottom, the lane bends sharply right, and passes a dwelling.

③ Go left at the T-junction and keep going until you reach **the Manor House**, with church and yew tree opposite. This three-storey grandiose dwelling, with double hipped tiled roof and half dormers, provided the inspiration for Edward Thomas' poem 'The Manor Farm'. Maintain direction past another house and then turn immediately left at a public footpath fingerpost.

Priors Dean church and yew

The Manor House, Priors Dean

Priors Dean is a small, scattered hamlet in an isolated rural area. There is no village hall or shop - only a Norman church and a large ancient yew. For some reason, the name 'Priors Dean' doesn't appear on OS maps!

4. Keep to left-hand edge of field on a rising path. When you reach the top left hand corner, go through a gap in the hedge into the next field. Maintain direction over the crest of the hill, keeping the hedge to your left.

5. At the top left-hand corner of the field, join a path that leads downhill through the hanger. When you reach the bottom, bear left at the junction, and then immediately right, at the yellow waymarked post.

6. When you emerge from woodland, it is not that obvious where the footpath leads. But maintain direction across field to the top right hand corner and locate an enclosed grassy lane. At end of lane, turn right along field edge, keeping line of oak trees to your left.

Approaching Hawkley Hanger

7. When you reach an unpaved lane, go left and then half-right, soon afterwards, across a stile and along an enclosed path between horse paddocks. Cross another stile and maintain direction down a narrow lane with high banks.

8. Turn right at the T-junction and follow road past **Hawkley church** and village green.

9. Pass the **Old Post Office** and then bear immediately right at the **Hangers Way** fingerpost. Keep to the right of the garage block, and proceed along the field edge. After entering woodland, turn right at fingerpost along the **Hangers Way**.

10 The path takes you along the right hand edge of Hawkley Hanger, where beech and yew woodland predominate. In the distance, there is the familiar outline of Noar Hill, shaped like a monk's head, with a corn field for a bald patch. After 700 metres, the path starts ascending and swings to the left and then to the right.

11 At the next waymarked junction, fork right along the **Hangers Way**. In due course the path emerges from woodland, with a field on the left hand side. Keep ahead at the next fingerpost, down a man-made staircase and then across a footbridge over a dried-up stream. Climb staircase and cross stile soon afterwards. Cut diagonally across field and cross stile in top right-hand corner.

12 Proceed along left-hand edge of next field. Climb stile (with three steps) at field corner and drop down to a lane. Turn left past a pond and maintain direction to the lay-by where the walk began.

View of Noar Hill from Button's Lane

5 Greatham and Empshott

A fascinating 5½ mile circuit that combines orchards with Greensand Hangers

Orchards are a key feature of this walk, and the ones you'll encounter are part of the Blackmoor Estate. During the 1920s, Lord Wolmer decided to establish a fruit farm at Blackmoor on the malmstone fields. Blackmoor Orchards now grow apples, pears, plums and soft fruit for many of the high street multiple retail outlets on 250 acres of orchards. The Blackmoor Farm Shop specializes in fresh fruit grown on the Estate's orchards: Cox, Red Pippen, Russets and Gala are some of the varieties of apple available.

Level: 🥾 🥾
Length: 5½ miles (8.8 km)
Terrain: Undulating field paths with an overgrown section between points 5 and 6; boots and long trousers recommended.
Park and start: Layby near St John the Baptist church, Greatham
Start ref: SU 773303
Postcode: GU33 6HD
Public transport: Bus 202 from Liss station (infrequent service) stops in Greatham
Refreshments and facilities:
The Grange Farm Shop, Empshott; the Greatham Inn, Greatham

The Manor House, Greatham

1 From the layby, walk past **St John the Baptist church, Greatham** and turn left down Church Lane. Keep following the lane as it bends sharp right, passing several houses.

Orchard near Squiresfield Hanger

St John the Baptist church, Greatham

> St John the Baptist church, Greatham was dedicated in 1875 and like most churches built during the religious fervour of the Victorian Age, was financed by a local family, the Fosters, who lived nearby at Le Court.

2 When the tarmac runs out, keep ahead into woodland. Cross over a small stream and continue along woodland edge with towering oak trees all around.

3 Climb stile and then go immediately left up a broad rising path across a field. Cross stile and proceed along path with hedge and ditch on left. Enter woodland and follow fence along edge of orchard. When you reach a gate, go right and then immediately left up **Squiresfield Hanger**. After a short climb, go right over stile and keep to left hand edge of field. Go through gate in field corner and along sunken lane.

(4) Turn left at the road, opposite **Bradshott Farm Cottage**, and proceed uphill for 300 metres. At crest of hill, go half right through metal kissing gate and follow fence along edge of orchard. After 200 metres, bear sharp right down hanger. Follow path as it turns sharp left through kissing gate. Great views open up of **Blackmoor church tower** in the distance. Proceed downhill along edge of field and across a broken stile. Go down man-made staircase to edge of lake. Cross another stile and follow path anticlockwise around lake and then through woodland. Climb stile on right and then proceed across field towards next stile.

(5) When you reach a wooden fingerpost, bear left with fence on right hand side. Go left at top of field, and keep woodland on right hand side. Proceed downhill through valley, passing another pool, with **Outshott and Adderhood Hanger** on left hand side. These steep wooded embankments, on the edge of the Malmstone escarpment, look man-made but are naturally occurring. At the end of the field, cross stile and proceed along edge of woodland, making a detour around any fallen trees. Ascend a small rise and when path peters out, continue across a stretch of rough overgrown terrain — probably the toughest part of the walk! At next waymark post, go down staircase and cross footbridge over stream. Keep going until you reach a road.

Signpost near lake

Autumn on Noar Hill

Field of horses near Noar Hill

6 Cross road and proceed up sunken tree-lined path towards Noar Hill. Keep following tree-lined path as it bends half left at top of field. When you reach a T-junction, go left along perimeter edge of **Noar Hill**. Keep following path which eventually bends round to the right and then meets a T-junction. Go left here, and then bear right over stile and across a field. Cross another stile and keep to right-hand edge of field.

Sign for Grange Farm Shop

The first Leonard Cheshire Home was established at Le Court in 1948 to care for people with disabilities. It was closed in 2007, due to changes in social services thinking in favour of 'care in the community'.

7 When you reach the road, bear right for a detour to **Grange Farm Shop** and **Empshott church**. To continue the walk bear left, and when you reach the main road, take footpath across a field. Climb a stile and then a double stile soon after. Keep going until you reach a lane. Walk towards a house, and then turn sharp right up a narrow tree-lined sunken path. Pass farm buildings on right and when the lane ends, join a metalled lane on left.

8 Maintain direction down a private road, passing a sign for **Laundry Cottage** and keep ahead at the next junction. Continue downhill until you reach the main road.

9 Turn obliquely left over a stile and then cut diagonally across a field. Climb stile in field corner, and proceed along path through woodland. Join an untarred lane, and keep going until you reach a road. Go right here and retrace your steps back to Greatham church.

Detail of stained glass window in Greatham church

The Swiss-based L'Abri Fellowship was founded in 1955 by Francis and Edith Schaeffer, who opened up their home as a spiritual shelter for those seeking answers to life's questions. The English branch of L'Abri is based at the Manor House, Greatham.

Beech tree in autumnal splendour

Lake near Outshott Hang

6 Noar Hill and Selborne Common

An enchanting 6 mile circuit that explores Selborne Common and the chalk pits of Noar Hill

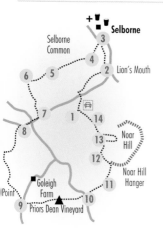

Level: 🥾 🥾
Length: 6 miles (9.5 km)
Terrain: Undulating, with one steep climb up Noar Hill
Park and start: Roadside verge at base of Noar Hill
Start ref: SU 738322
Postcode: GU34 3LW
Public transport: None to start, but Stagecoach bus (number 72) from Alton to Petersfield station stops outside the Selborne Arms
Refreshments and facilities:
The Tea Parlour at Gilbert White's House; the Queens, Selborne; the Selborne Arms

Noar Hill was once the site of medieval chalk pits, but is now carpeted with flowering plants and downland grasses. Yew trees and ragged juniper bushes also thrive on the grassed-over chalk pits. Managed by Hampshire Wildlife Trust, this unusual landscape has over a dozen species of orchids, including the rare Musk orchid. The strong populations of cowslips during the spring are a food source for the caterpillars of The Duke of Burgundy butterfly.

Bridleway on Noar Hill

View from the top of the Zig Zag Path

3 Turn left just before you reach the car park along a path signposted the Zig Zag Path. Proceed along an enclosed path and through a kissing gate to ascend the **Zig Zag Path**. Savour the outstanding views of the village and surrounding area, and when you reach the top, bear half right and head for a kissing gate which leads to Selborne Common.

1 Proceed along lane in a northerly direction and at road junction, keep ahead over a stile. Cut diagonally right across a field to a V-shaped stile, and along a grassy track. Go through another V-shaped stile and along the right hand edge of a field. Cross another stile and proceed along the edge of a second field.

2 Follow the green **Hangers Way** arrow over another stile and down a narrow path, which merges with a metalled lane. Follow this lane all the way to the **Selborne Arms car park**.

Autumn on Selborne Common

Umbellifer on the top of Button's Lane

(4) Keep on the obvious path, through woodland, scrub and open areas. When you reach a clearing with gorse stands, the track divides.

(5) Take the left fork on a steadily descending path.

(6) When you come to a stile and a gate, go left and then immediately right downhill, at a wooden fingerpost. Keep on this steadily descending path, which soon becomes a sunken lane. To the left there are fabulous views of Noar Hill.

(7) When you reach a road, bear right and keep ahead at the next crossroads. After a few hundred metres, you reach a passing point.

(8) Bear left along a narrow tree-lined avenue (not waymarked). Continue on a steadily ascending path, which eventually emerges from woodland. The track veers sharply to the left, then to the right and back to the left again, before reaching a road. It's worth stopping here to admire the spectacular views on offer from this hilltop vantage point.

View of Noar Hill from sunken lane

9 Go straight ahead along a metalled lane. When the road goes right into a farm, keep ahead down a heavily-wooded sunken lane. Pass **Priors Dean Vineyard** on the right, before reaching a road.

10 Zig zag left and then right over a stile to follow the Hangers Way. Keep to the left hand edge of the first field, and follow the well-worn path across the second field. Climb the stile which leads to a road.

Hangers Way signpost near Noar Hill

Bent signpost near Button's Lane

11 Go right to ford a small stream and then left over a stile (Hangers Way). After 50 metres, bear half right over an unusual stile and across a field. Climb another stile into dense woodland. Continue on a very steep path up a wooded hanger.

Noar Hill is a favoured habitat for Glow-worms, Rufous Grasshoppers and the bizarre Fairy Shrimp, which lives in ephemeral pools on rutted tracks.

12 When you come to a finger-post and a complex junction, keep ahead along a tree-lined path which bisects a corn field. Pass through a kissing gate bearing a sign for Noar Hill.

13 Go right at the next fingerpost and when you reach a bench and another fingerpost, turn obliquely left along a grassy track. Keep going until you pass an area of **grassed-over chalk pits**, with a small turquoise information board on the left. Maintain direction and descend into the hollow of a large chalk pit. Some of this area may be cordoned off with electrified fencing, if cattle are grazing. Notice the yew trees and

Grassed-over chalk pit on Noar Hill

ragged juniper bushes, as you come to a clearing, with views towards Selborne Hanger. Maintain direction to a kissing gate.

14 Bear left along this track and when you reach a metalled lane, go left to parking area on road-side verge.

Chalk pit amphitheatre

7 Selborne Hanger and the Long Lythe

A classic 4½ mile circuit in Gilbert White country, taking in Selborne Hanger and the Long Lythe

The village of Selborne lies on a narrow Greensand plateau with Chalk hangers to the west and the Greensand hangers to the east. Its most celebrated inhabitant was the 18th century naturalist and clergyman Gilbert White, author of the *Natural History of Selborne*, and founding father of natural history recording. At one time, the above work was the fourth most published book in the English Language – after the Bible, Shakespeare and the Oxford English Dictionary. Combining scientific journalism, with parish record and sacred poetry, the book doesn't fit comfortably into any category. Writers as diverse as Darwin, Coleridge, and Auden have all paid their tributes.

The Queens, Selborne

Level: 🥾

Length: 4½ miles (7.2 km)

Terrain: One moderate ascent up Selborne Hanger and then along field paths and waymarked tracks

Park and start: Selborne Arms car park

Start ref: SU 742335

Postcode: GU34 3JR

Public transport: Stagecoach bus (number 72) from Alton to Petersfield railway station stops outside the Selborne Arms

Refreshments and facilities:
The Tea Parlour at Gilbert White's House; the Queens, Selborne; the Selborne Arms

43

1. Locate the information board in the car park, and then take the path obliquely right, past the toilet block, waymarked the **Zig Zag Path**. Go down a narrow enclosed path and through a kissing gate . Bear left and ascend the Zig Zag Path up **Selborne Hanger**, cut by Gilbert White and his brother in 1753. As you ascend the path, fabulous views open up of **Wick Hill Farm** and **Milking Hanger** (on the hill opposite) and the 'white golf balls' of **RAF Oakhanger**. Two thirds of the way up there is a metal bench. Keep going and when you reach the top, bear right and then right again to follow the path along the edge of the hanger.

The Wakes from the Zig Zag Path

The Oates Museum commemorates the Oates family and their exploits, and in particular Captain Lawrence Oates, who accompanied Scott to the South Pole in 1911.

2 Good views of **Selborne village** and '**The Wakes**' open up through the trees to your right. Continue along the edge of the hanger past towering beeches with pendulous boughs.

Selborne village from the hanger

3 When you reach a metal bench, keep ahead, ignoring the path off to the right. Stop here to savour spectacular views of **Selborne church** and the '**The Wakes**' with **Wick Hill Farm** and **Milking Hanger** behind it. Continue along a narrow descending path, which eventually meets a gulley and a dried-up pit. When you reach a T-junction, go right and continue round a sharp left hand bend.

4 Turn left at the road, passing several houses, and take the next right up a farm track. Cross a stile and proceed along the left hand edge of the field. When you reach the top left-hand corner, keep ahead across the next field to a stile.

5 Fork right here across a field to cross a slab footbridge into another field. Keep to the left hand edge of the field, on a rising path. Half way up a sunken stream-bed will appear to the left of the path.

In the 1930s, there were at least five hop gardens around Ketchers, owned by the Blackmoor estate. During the hop-picking season, Selborne was a ghost village, with parents and children alike, both working in the hop fields.

6 At the road, go straight across, up a concrete farm track, keeping the stream on the left. When the left-hand hedge disappears, maintain direction across field. When you reach the end, locate a fingerpost, and keep ahead along a sunken path. Proceed along right hand edge of field, with beech, birch, hazel and ash woodland of **Milking Hanger** to your right. Pass **Wick Hill Cottage** on the left and turn right when you reach a metalled lane.

7 When the tarmac ends, continue past **Wick Hill Farm** and through a farm gate. The track soon becomes a sunken lane, with loose boulders underfoot. Go through a metal gate, and follow left-hand fence, as it veers sharp left (at the blue waymark).

Path to Wick Hill Farm

8 Cross a stile and bear right along a deeply rutted woodland track, which veers to the left and then goes downhill.

Selborne Priory was founded by the Bishop of Winchester in 1233. For 250 years it marked time inconspicuously and then collapsed in scandal in 1484. Magdalen College asked for its closure and property, which was confirmed by papal bull in 1486.

Detail from St Francis window in Selborne church

9 Just before you reach the pond at **Priory Farm**, go right through a metal kissing gate. Keep to right hand edge of field, and cross stile into woodland. Climb another stile and proceed across field and past three ponds.

10 Go through kissing gate into the **Long Lythe**, and keep following the green Hangers Way arrow. Go through two more kissing gates, and just before you reach houses, note the Upper Greensand (Malmstone) rock outcrop on the embankment to your right.

Gilbert White acquired his pet tortoise, Timothy, from his widowed aunt, Mrs Rebecca Snooke, who lived in Ringmer, Sussex. The tortoise is reputed to have lived to a grand old age of 64.

11 Cross a footbridge and proceed up a sloping field (**Church Meadow**) to the far end of Selborne churchyard. Pass **Selborne church** with its spectacular stained glass windows, dedicated to the memory of Gilbert White. Cross **The Plestor** and then bear left up Selborne high street, past '**The Wakes**', **the Queens** and **the Selborne Arms**, back to the car park.
The Long Lythe in autumn

The Lion's Mouth

The trunk of the great yew tree in Selborne churchyard is estimated to be 1,400 years old. When it blew down in 1990, it measured 8 metres in girth, and was taller than the church.

8 Chawton and West Worldham

An exhilarating 9½ mile hike across Jane Austen country, taking in Farringdon and West Worldham

Jane Austen spent the last eight years of her life (1809 -1817) at Chawton, writing and revising her great 'romantic comedies'. *Pride and Prejudice, Sense and Sensibility* and *Northanger Abbey* were all revised for press here, and three more novels were completed: *Mansfield Park, Emma* and *Persuasion*. Jane was careful that her occupation should not be suspected by anyone outside her own family circle. She wrote on small sheets of paper which could easily be put away, or covered with a piece of blotting paper.

Level: 🥾 🥾 🥾
Length: 9½ miles (15.3 km)
Terrain: Mainly flat walking across fields and farmland
Park and start: Chawton village car park
Start ref: SU 709375
Postcode: GU34 1SE
Public transport: Stagecoach bus (number 72) from Alton to Petersfield stops at Chawton, opposite the Grey Friar Inn
Refreshments and facilities:
The Grey Friar Inn, Chawton;
Cassandra's Cup teashop;
the Rose and Crown, Upper Farringdon

Jane Austen's House
Kiln House 15
1
17
16
2
14
B3006
West Worldham
Greencroft Cottage
9
13
8
Dismantled Railway
7
10
6
Malmstone escarpment
12
3
Site of Medieval
Village of
Hartley Mauditt
11
5
Lower
Farringdon
4
Upper Farringdon

The Rose and Crown, Upper Farringdon

Jane Austen's House

1 From **Jane Austen's House** and the **Grey Friar Inn**, proceed along lane past Chawton recreation ground. Take the first right at the wooden fingerpost along **Ferney Close**. Pass between houses, then cross stile to follow **St Swithun's Way**.

2 Climb a high stile, cross main road, then up some steps and over another stile. Follow hedgerow, then bear left over stile into copse. Bear right at the fingerpost and then left. After a field length, you join the now disused Meon Valley railway line. Follow this tree-lined track as far as it goes (approx.1.5km), then bear left along footpath to road.

Massey's Folly, Farringdon

3 Go straight across busy **A32**, and proceed uphill along byway. Keep ahead at junction near houses, go through farmyard, and turn right when you reach Manor Farm house. Pass the lych-gate of **All Saints' church** on the left and bear right at road. Proceed past **Massey's Folly** (now the village hall), made from red brick and terracotta tiles; continue along road which bends sharp left and then up a gentle incline.

Massey's Folly was the eccentric idea of the Reverend Thomas Massey – a former rector of Farringdon. Employing just three tradesmen, he spent 30 years constructing the folly from red brick and terracotta tiles.

4 Bear left at junction in the direction of **Selborne**. Keep ahead at next junction along a narrow alleyway, with **Rose and Crown car park** on left. Keep following the left hand hedgerow as it zig zags left and then right.

5 Pass under pylon, and then turn immediately left at wooden sign (with missing fingerpost).

Continue along right hand hedgerow to field corner, then bear right (at yellow arrow) across two small footbridges. Keep ahead (i.e. south easterly direction) towards row of pylons. Bear left at end of field and follow right hand hedgerow, until you reach a concealed footbridge on right. Cross it and pass to the left of a small pond.

6 Continue under pylons in direction of large tree and two galvanized gates. Climb stile near gates, and cross concrete footbridge. Walk uphill with brook on right hand side to top of field. Cross footbridge, and cut diagonally left across field to another footbridge. Keep steadily ascending until you reach a main road.

Pit near Farringdon

Approaching West Worldham

7 Go left and then right at wooden fingerpost towards white house in the distance. Follow hedgerow round to the left and keep ahead at the next field corner. Turn immediately right and follow right hand hedge to a road.

8 Turn left and at the next 90 degree bend, go right along a farm track. Pass **Little Pullens** and when the track peters out, keep ahead across a large field (aiming for a solitary oak). When you reach the top of the field, go left and locate a three way signpost. You are now standing on the edge of Warner's Hanger.

9 Bear right and descend the hanger via a sunken path. At the bottom, climb a stile and then bear right through a gate and continue along muddy track to a road. Cross it and then bear immediately right up a man-made staircase.

10 At the top of Park Hanger, go left and maintain direction to the field corner. If you wish to view an outcrop of Upper Greensand (or Malmstone) on the banks of the sunken lane below, make a short diversion left.

11 To continue the walk, keep to the edge of the field as it bends right. Keep following the embanked serpentine path (with a sunken lane to your left) for about

1 Km. Go left at the next wooden fingerpost and when you reach a road, turn right along it.

12 Pass **Hartley Pond** and **St Leonard's church, Hartley Mauditt**, and maintain direction towards **West Worldham**. Pass a thatched cottage on the right, and when you reach a road junction (near **Greencroft Cottage**), bear left along

St Leonard's church, Hartley Mauditt was built between 1100 and 1125 by one of William the Conqueror's knights, William de Mauditt. It is the only building left standing of the former village of Hartley Mauditt.

a footpath (point 8). Follow a hedge and then keep to the left of a small spinney.

13 Go straight over a road, cross another field and when you reach a metal gate, climb over it and follow right-hand hedgerow. Pass under two sets of pylons and as you approach two belts of woodland, move to the left hand side of the field and locate a stile.

14 Cross stile and maintain direction towards farm buildings, with stream on right. Pass tennis court on left hand side and walk across meadow towards **Kiln Farm**. Go through metal gate, cross stile and across footbridge to metalled lane.

St Leonard's church, Hartley Mauditt

53

15 Turn left, cross bridge and then bear right at next finger-post. Climb stile, cross footbridge and follow path to farm buildings. Turn sharp left at yellow arrow and follow path to a road.

16 Go straight across, through kissing gate and along wide farm track. Turn sharp right through gate, and pass small pit on right hand side. Go through another metal gate, and bear half right towards a double stile. Proceed towards distant farm buildings, climb stile, and when you reach farm, go right along lane and then immediately left across a field with cattle.

17 Follow the obvious path towards woodland. Go through kissing gate and down incline. Climb two more stiles across horse paddocks and head towards metal kissing gate. Follow narrow alleyway to road. Bear left towards **Jane Austen's House** and car park.

One of the exhibits in Jane Austen's House is the creaking swing door in the drawing room, which gave her notice of servants or visitors approaching. When the hinges creaked, she discretely hid her papers away.

Kiln Farm

9 Oakhanger and East Worldham

A diverse 7 mile circuit along the edge of the Malmstone escarpment and past the 'white golf balls' of RAF Oakhanger

North of Selborne, the Upper Greensand escarpment becomes more prominent than the Chalk escarpment. Upper Greensand is a sandstone

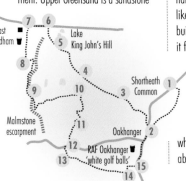

that varies from soft sand to a hard, pale-coloured calcareous sandstone, known as Malmstone — one of the hardest rocks in Hampshire. It looks like chalk, and has long been the chief building material in the area; however, it frequently needs to be reinforced with brickwork, particularly around windows and doors. One of the finest views of the Malmstone escarpment is along the route from Oakhanger to East Worldham, where the shelf rises spectacularly above the landscape.

Lakes near East Worldham

Level: 🐾 🐾
Length: 7 miles (11.2 km)
Terrain: Delightfully varied - across fields, through pine woods and along edge of Malmstone escarpment
Park and start: Shortheath Common car park
Start ref: SU 775369
Postcode (nearest): GU35 9HE
Public transport: None to start , but bus 212 goes from Alton to Oakhanger (infrequent service)
Refreshments and facilities:
The Three Horseshoes, East Worldham; the Red Lion, Oakhanger

1 From **Shortheath Common car park**, go clockwise around the lake, and then keep going in a south-westerly direction across the common. Maintain direction as a wide track merges from the left and then cross a clearing. When you reach a tarmac drive, go right towards the church.

Footbridge near St John's Hill

Shortheath Common

2 Take the road to the right of **St Mary Magdalene** church, turn sharp right and follow alleyway to the left of the garage block. At the next junction, bear left along a wide farm track. To the left you will see the '**white golf balls**' of RAF Oakhanger and behind it the treed ridge of the Malmstone escarpment.

Path near Malmstone escarpment

3 When you reach a cottage, keep ahead over a stile into woodland. Keep on main track through the wood, cross a clearing and when the wood ends continue to a fingerpost.

4 Go over footbridge and through kissing gate. Aim slightly to the left of **King John's Hill** and go through two more kissing gates in quick succession. Pass through another gate to enter woodland and proceed up a broad rising path that swings sharp left at the top. Go through gate and follow avenue of trees over shoulder of hill, towards two lakes.

5 Go left before first lake, at a green Hangers Way arrow and negotiate another kissing gate. Go half right across field in direction of farmhouse. Bear right when you reach a metalled farm track and continue to main road.

6 Cross road then turn left along it. Pass layby in front of **village hall**, and keep ahead if you wish to make a detour to **the Three Horseshoes pub** (recommended).

7 To continue walk, take the first footpath left after layby, up a concrete staircase. Cross stile and continue along right hand edge of field, passing a **hop kiln** conversion. Climb stile and continue along enclosed path behind house. Cross metalled lane and maintain direction past a barn along right hand edge of field.

Path out of East Worldham

8 Go sharp left at broken fingerpost and follow left hand edge of next field. Go right at field corner and continue along edge of the **Malmstone escarpment**. Notice how steep the slope is from the top of the hanger to the fields below. Keep ahead into the next field and pass a large pylon.

View of 'white golf balls' from malmstone escarpment

9 Turn obliquely left, soon after, and descend **Warner's Hanger** via the sunken path. At the bottom, climb stile and then bear right along field edge to a gate and along muddy track to a road. Turn left past chalet and house and keep ahead along byway into woodland. The track widens out and becomes increasingly rutted and occasionally fallen trees block the path.

Steps up Ridge Hanger

10 After 800 metres, bear sharp right into woodland at an easily-missed (low-level) Hangers Way signpost. The track soon broadens out and becomes a woodland ride. Go through kissing gate and then cut half right across a clearing to another gate. Continue along woodland ride with giant fir trees on right. Turn sharp left and go clockwise around pool.

11 At next major junction, zig zag left and then right to follow Hangers Way up a wide woodland ride. Track continues to rise and then bears half left. Keep going until you reach a metalled lane.

12 Go right here and then left soon after along the Hangers Way. Pass **High Candovers** and a few dwellings.

13 After thatched barn, go half left through gate, along woodland edge. Go through gate, over a track, and continue along woodland ride, which eventually swings to the left. Cross a wide track then a stile and continue along right hand edge of field, with the **'white golfballs'** now in view to your left. At the end of the field, cross a footbridge and a stile.

The 'white golf balls' of RAF Oakhanger are fibre glass domes that protect the large satellite dishes used to receive data from military and civilian satellites. The land was bought by the War Department in 1938, because the bowl-shaped terrain made the area electrically quiet.

14 Go half left across field, aiming for 'white golf balls'. Go through 'hedge' and maintain direction towards top right hand corner of next field. Climb double stile, then bear left along edge of field. Follow it until you reach a stile and a thatched house (**Tunford**) near a main road.

15 Cross road and go left along it into Oakhanger village and past the **Red Lion pub**. When the pavement runs out, walk carefully along road for approx.100 metres. Take the next right (point 2), up a driveway opposite the church and retrace your steps across Shortheath Common back to the car park.

Close-up of 'white golf ball'

Thatched house in Oakhanger

10 Binsted, Wyck and Wheatley

Explore the 'northern hangers' on this 4¾ mile walk across the 'Binsted peninsula'

Binsted was once the centre of a prosperous hop-growing industry, as is evident from the numerous hop kiln conversions now in the area. Hops were dried immediately after harvesting and the kilns operated constantly, to keep up with the picking. Hops were then sold to local breweries who added them to beer to produce the distinctive bitterness. It was the Malmstone geology of the 'Binsted peninsula' that provided the fertile soil on which to grow hops.

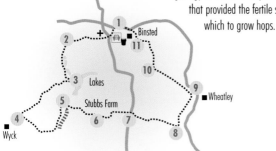

Level:
Length: 4¾ miles (7.6 km)
Terrain: Undulating field paths and sunken lanes
Park and start: The Cedars pub car park, Binsted (patrons only)
Start ref: SU 773411
Postcode: GU34 4PB
Public transport: Countryliner coach (C44) runs from Alton to Binsted
Refreshments and facilities:
The Cedars pub, Binsted

*East end of Binsted
Holy Cross church*

1 With your back to **the Cedars pub**, go left along the road. Bear left at the first fingerpost and take enclosed path across fields. When you reach **Binsted Holy Cross church**, keep ahead through church gate. After passing church tower, keep

Hop kiln conversion in Wyck

to the right hand edge of churchyard. Pass grave of Field Marshal Montgomery, and continue along right hand edge of next field. Follow the hedge as it bends right and then go immediately left across another field.

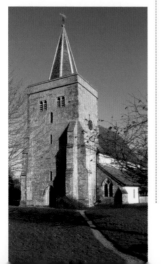

Field Marshal Montgomery ('Monty') – one of the most famous soldiers of World War II – is buried in Binsted churchyard. He successfully commanded Allied Forces at Alamein and directed the invasion of the Normandy beaches on D-Day.

Binsted Holy Cross churchyard

2 Drop down into gulley and cross a footbridge. Bear left along path and maintain direction for 600 metres past two large lakes.

3 When you reach a sunken lane, go right up a rising path. Ignore left turn to conservation area and follow sunken lane uphill and past houses on left.

(4) Just afterwards, gain the road and turn left in the direction of **Wyck Farmhouse**. Pass hop kiln conversion on right hand side, then go left at next fingerpost, along track to dwellings. Go through gate into conservation area, and follow footpath along left hand edge of field. When you reach a fingerpost, keep ahead along right hand edge of next field. Keep going along the gently-sloped edge of the Malmstone escarpment.

(5) Go right at the next fingerpost and descend the hanger, via a man-made staircase. At the bottom, keep ahead in the direction of power lines. Cross a footbridge, and follow the rising path across a field. When you reach woodland, continue along left hand edge of field.

Fingerpost at Stubbs Farm

(6) At **Stubbs Farm**, zig zag left and then right through farmyard. Follow metalled lane out of farm with great views of Binsted church tower to the left. Path meanders left and then right before reaching a road.

(7) Go straight across, past **Garden Cottage** and **Colesons**, up a rising path. Keep ahead across field to a stile. Cross another field and climb second stile. Maintain direction on a rising path over crest of hill. Descend to a small waymarked post at end of field.

8 Go left along edge of field, with great views to the right of **Alice Holt Forest**.

9 When you reach houses, go left along a farm track and across fields. Keep going until you reach a barn, made from white Malmstone.

10 Here the track swings sharp right and eventually crosses a sunken stream and a belt of woodland.

11 At the road, go right up a sunken lane, which has eroded downwards to reveal gnarled tree roots and exposures of Malmstone geology. Turn left at the main road and continue through Binsted village to **the Cedars pub**.

Approaching Whea